BEANO
ULTIMATE JOKE BOOK

First published in the UK in 2018 by Studio Press
An imprint of Kings Road Publishing
Part of Bonnier Books UK
The Plaza, 535 King's Road,
London, SW10 0SZ
Owned by Bonnier Books,
Sveavägen 56, Stockholm, Sweden

www.studiopressbooks.co.uk

www.beano.com

A Beano Studios Product © D.C. Thomson & Co. Ltd 2018

A CIP catalogue record for this book
is available from the British Library.

Paperback: 978-1-78741-156-2

Printed and bound by Clays Ltd, Elcograf S.p.A.

8 10 9 7

Studio Press is an imprint of Bonnier Books UK
www.bonnierbooks.co.uk

Written by Kay Woodward
Edited by Frankie Jones
Designed by Deryck Tilling
Cover design by Rob Ward

BEANO
ULTIMATE
JOKE
BOOK

For Gnasher

Please laugh
at these jokes.
I will pay you.

DENNIS

CONTENTS

Dear trainee comedian,

The *Beano* has been funny FOREVER. OK, since 1938. But that's practically prehistory, which means that Dennis, Minnie the Minx and the Bash Street Kids have had oodles of practice in being hilarious. They're comics from a comic!

Geddit? Ha haaaaa! See? Utterly hilarious.

So here's the deal. Because we love nothing more than a good joke at *Beano**, we decided to create *the ULTIMATE Joke Book*, so you can be funny, too. And guess what? Now that you've bought this book, you're in!

By reading this amazing joke book, you'll learn how to be a real, true-life comedian. What sort of a joker are you? Whizz to page 10 to find out! Then scoot to page 12 to learn how to tell a joke. Finally, flip to page 14 for insider tips on how to write your very own comedy masterpieces.

And that's not all! Starting on page 17, there's premium access to **over 600 jokes** to kick-start your comedy career. Dinosaur jokes? Tick. Monster jokes? Tick. Animal, bug, under-the-sea, Christmas, Doctor-Doctor, food, knock-knock, music, school, space and sports jokes? A GAZILLION TICKS. There's even a collection of jokes so totally silly that you'll read them and weep (with laughter, obvs).

Ha-ha-ha-happy joking!

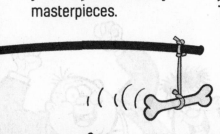

*except perhaps a world-class prank involving Walter and a bucket of custard.

HOW TO BE A COMEDIAN

It's EASY. You've just got to be funny, right?

Well, yes. But before you even start cracking jokes, you'll need to develop your comedy persona. Relax! Comedy persona is just a fancy way of describing what you're like in front of an audience. And before you go out and buy a clown suit and learn how to cartwheel, STOP. There's only one thing you need to develop your comedy persona... and that's YOU.

Being a stand-up comedian isn't like being an actor. You don't need to pretend to be someone else. You just need to be yourself, but a little larger than life. (Sadly, this isn't an excuse to eat 36 doughnuts.) Do you have a voice like a foghorn? Then turn up the volume! Are you a chatterbox? Chatter more! Do you wave your arms around enthusiastically when you speak? GO REALLY WILD!

There's no need to dress up either, unless you want to. Sure, some comedians always wear the same thing, like a fez or a moustache or a shirt with a huuuuuge collar. So if there's something you love to wear – like, say, a red-and-black-striped jumper – then wear that. But don't worry about it too much. Because the thing you need to concentrate on being is YOURSELF.

HOW TO BE FUNNY

Grab your comedy lab coat! It's time for the super-duper scientific bit… *drumroll*… how to be funny. And not just a little bit funny, either. Our top-secret formula will help you to be so side-splittingly hilarious that you'll be able to make a teacher laugh. (Maybe even a HEAD TEACHER.)

Because there's a lot more to telling a joke than just reading it out… you can use:

THE FUNNY FORMULA

RELAX. Smile. Imagine your best friend just sat on a whoopee cushion. If you're in a good mood, your audience will be, too. They'll be ready to laugh!

GIVE IT OOMPH. Make sure that your voice goes up and down as you speak to bring your joke to life. Add a pinch of pzazz! A sprinkling of zing! The last thing you want to do is sound as if you're reading the newzzzzzz…

STOP. Before you deliver the punchline – the funny bit at the end of the joke – pause for a second. Then your audience will be on the edge of their seats, wondering what you're going to say next. It'll make them *even more ready* to laugh.

WAIT. Yayyyyyy! you're a comedy genius. You've delivered the punchline and your audience is rolling in the aisles! They're clutching their sides! They're crying with laughter! And here's the important part: pause before rushing on with your next joke. Give the crowd a chance to laugh. If you tell another joke now, they won't hear you. Besides, laughing is FUN. So let them guffaw and giggle and chortle and chuckle for a few seconds before blasting them with your next comedy masterpiece.

RELAX + GIVE IT OOMPH + STOP + WAIT = MEGALOLZ

HOW TO WRITE YOUR OWN JOKES

Here at *Beano* HQ, we're so incredibly kind and considerate that we've stuffed the rest of this book with ready-made jokes, just for you. (And, erm, anyone else who bought the book.) But if you're going to be the funniest kid on the block, you can go one better. You can write your own brand-new and 100% original gags! Here's how...

A joke is a story or a question followed by a punchline. All you have to do is make sure that the punchline makes sense but is something your audience doesn't expect. Like this:

What's green, hairy and goes up and down?

A gooseberry stuck in a lift.

(BONUS PUNCHLINE: *A kiwi fruit on a trampoline.*)

A top way of writing jokes is to use words that are spelled or pronounced the same, but have more than one meaning.

Like this:

Why was Cinderella such a rubbish netball player?

She kept running away from the ball.

The joke works because the word ball can mean both round, bouncy object AND a fancy party with posh frocks and lots of dancing. The audience expects the first meaning, but laughs when they realise there's actually a second meaning. (PS Never try to explain a joke. It stops being funny AT ONCE. See?)

And remember the stupendously silly jokes like this:

What colour is a burp?

Burple.

Psst! There's room at the end of this book to write down your own jokes!

WARNING:
These jokes are so ~~bad~~ brilliant that your friends will be begging you ~~to stop~~ for more.

ANIMAL JOKES

IT'S TIME TO HEE-HAW LIKE A DONKEY, HONK LIKE A GOOSE, LAUGH LIKE A HYENA, HOWL LIKE A MONKEY AND GROAN LIKE A WALRUS AT THESE **BEAR**-ILLIANT JOKES.

MOO-VE ALONG NOW.

YOU'D BE **QUACKERS** NOT TO.

WHAT DO YOU CALL AN ELEPHANT
IN A PHONE BOX?

STUCK!

WHAT DO COWS READ IN
THE MORNING?

THE **MOOS**-PAPER!

WHAT IS IT CALLED WHEN A CAT WINS
A DOG SHOW?

A **CAT-HAS-TROPHY**!

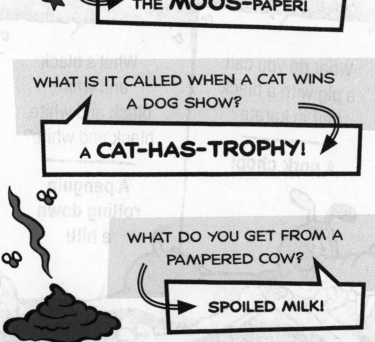

WHAT DO YOU GET FROM A
PAMPERED COW?

SPOILED MILK!

ANIMAL JOKES

How do dogs train their fleas?

From scratch!

Why did the bird go to the hospital?

To get tweet-ment!

What do you call a pig with a black belt in karate?

A pork chop!

What's black and white, black and white, black and white?

A penguin rolling down a hill!

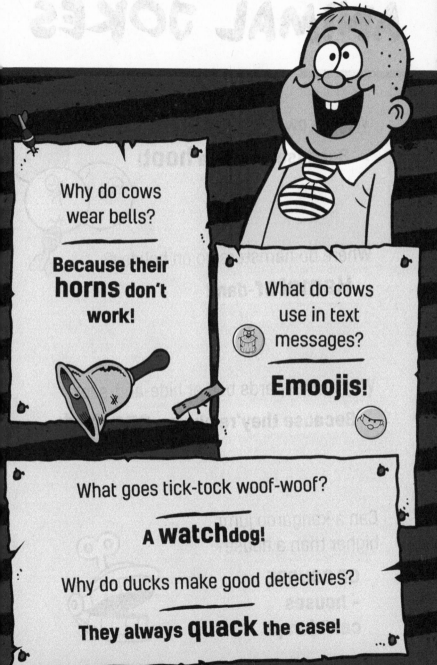

Why do cows wear bells?

Because their horns don't work!

What do cows use in text messages?

Emoojis!

What goes tick-tock woof-woof?

A **watch**dog!

Why do ducks make good detectives?

They always **quack** the case!

ANIMAL JOKES

Why do owls get invited to parties?

Because they're a hoot!

Where do hamsters go on holiday?

Hamster-dam!

Why are leopards bad at hide-and-seek?

Because they're always spotted!

Can a kangaroo jump higher than a house?

OF COURSE – houses can't jump!

What's the stupidest animal in the jungle?

The polar bear!

What do elephants wear
to go swimming?

Trunks!

What do you call a
sleeping bull?

A **bull**-dozer!

What do you get if you cross
a centipede with a parrot?

A **walkie-talkie!**

ANIMAL JOKES

WHY DID THE CHICKEN CROSS
THE PLAYGROUND?

TO GET TO THE OTHER SLIDE!

WHAT'S BLUE
AND HAS
BIG EARS?

**AN ELEPHANT AT
THE NORTH POLE!**

WHAT DO
HEDGEHOGS EAT?

PRICKLED
ONIONS!

HOW DOES A FARMER
COUNT THEIR ANIMALS?

WITH A COW-CULATOR!

WHY CAN'T YOU TALK TO A GOAT?

IT ALWAYS **BUTTS** IN!

WHERE DO COWS GO ON SATURDAY NIGHT?

TO THE **MOO**-VIES!

WHY DID THE BIRD FLY INTO THE LIBRARY?

BECAUSE IT WAS LOOKING FOR **BOOKWORMS!**

WHAT DO YOU CALL A DEER WITH NO EYES?

NO-EYE DEER!

ANIMAL JOKES

How does a mouse feel after a bath?

Squeaky-clean!

Why do cats have minty breath?

They use mouse-wash!

What colour do cats like?

Purr-ple!

WHAT DO YOU CALL A TIGER AT THE NORTH POLE?

LOST!

WHAT DID ONE PENGUIN SAY TO THE OTHER?

NOTHING, IT GAVE THEM THE COLD SHOULDER!

What's the difference between an orange and a walrus?

Give it a squeeze. If you don't get orange juice, it's a walrus!

What happened when the frog's car broke down?

It got toad away!

Why will a dog never win a dance competition?

It has two left feet!

ANIMAL JOKES

WHICH REPTILE
TELLS JOKES?

A STAND-UP
CHAMELEON!

WHAT DO YOU GET
IF YOU CROSS A DOG
WITH A CALCULATOR?

A BEST FRIEND
YOU CAN REALLY
COUNT ON!

WHAT DO YOU CALL
DOGS THAT DIG UP
ANCIENT ARTEFACTS?

BARK-AEOLOGISTS!

WHAT'S A DOG'S
FAVOURITE KIND
OF PIZZA?

PUP-ERONI!

WHAT KIND OF DOG IS GOOD AT MAGIC TRICKS?

A LABRACADABRADOR!

WHAT DO WOLVES SAY WHEN THEY MEET?

HOWL DO YOU DO?

WHAT KIND OF DOG COMES FROM ASGARD AND WIELDS A MIGHTY HAMMER?

A LABRA-**THOR**!

WHAT DO YOU CALL IT WHEN ONE COW SPIES ON ANOTHER?

A **STEAK**-OUT!

ANIMAL JOKES

WHAT'S A FROG'S FAVOURITE SWEET?

A LOLLI-**HOP!**

WHERE DO YOU TAKE SICK PONIES?

TO THE **HORSE**-PITAL!

HOW DO HEDGEHOGS PLAY LEAPFROG?

VERY, VERY CAREFULLY!

WHY DID THE BOA CONSTRICTORS GET MARRIED?

THEY HAD A **CRUSH** ON EACH OTHER!

WHAT GOES DOT-DASH-RIBBIT?

A MORSE **TOAD**!

WHAT DO YOU CALL A BEAR WITH NO TEETH?

A **GUMMY** BEAR!

WHAT GOES 'HITH, HITH'?

A SNAKE THAT'S BITTEN ITS TONGUE!

WHAT DO YOU GET IF YOU CROSS
AN ELEPHANT WITH A SPARROW?

BROKEN TELEPHONE WIRES!

ANIMAL JOKES

Why did the lion spit out the clown?

They tasted funny!

How do chickens communicate?

With fowl language!

Did you hear about the dog that ate nothing but garlic?

Its bark was worse than its bite!

What's the difference between an elephant and a biscuit?

You can't dip an elephant in your tea!

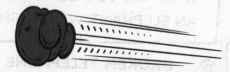

What do you get if you put a duck in a cement mixer?

Quacks in the pavement!

How do you make a baby snake cry?

Take its **rattle** away!

What do you call a pig that can't mind its own business?

A nosy porker!

Where do frogs hang their coats?

In the **croak**-room!

ANIMAL JOKES

WHAT DO YOU CALL TWO BIRDS IN LOVE?

TWEET-HEARTS!

WHAT DID ONE BAT SAY TO ANOTHER?

I LOVE HANGING AROUND WITH YOU!

WHAT DID THE SQUIRREL SAY TO THEIR FRIEND?

I'M **NUTS** ABOUT YOU!

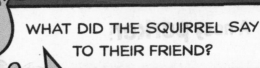

WHAT DO MICE HATE DOING MOST?

MOUSE-WORK!

WHAT'S A FROG'S FAVOURITE DRINK?

CROAKA-COLA!

WHAT DO YOU GET IF YOU CROSS A
SNAKE WITH A BUILDER?

A **BOA** CONSTRUCTOR!

WHAT DO YOU CALL A DONKEY
WITH THREE LEGS?

A WONKEY!

WHAT DO YOU DO IF YOU FIND A
BEAR IN YOUR TOILET?

LET THEM FINISH!

ANIMAL JOKES

Did you hear about the hungry lion?

They swallowed their pride!

What did Smiffy call his pet tiger?

Spot!

What's an alligator's favourite game?

Snap!

Why was the bear spoiled?

People always panda'd to him!

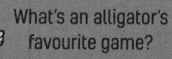

What snakes do you find on cars?
Windscreen vipers!

Why do cows lie down in groups when it's cold?
To keep each udder warm!

When does a duck get up?
At the quack of dawn!

What do cats have for breakfast?
Mice Krispies!

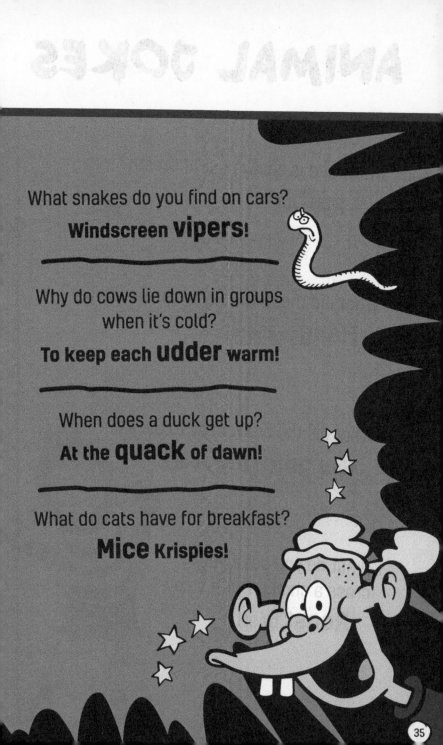

ANIMAL JOKES

What bird is always out of breath?

A puffin!

What did the nurse say to the poorly bat?

Hang in there!

What did the beaver say to the tree?

Nice gnawing you!

What do you get if you cross a chicken with a cow?

Roost beef!

What's a prickly pear?

Two hedgehogs!

What do you get if you cross a
hedgehog with a giraffe?

A really long toothbrush!

What do you get if you sit under a cow?

A pat on the head!

How do hens dance?

Chick to chick!

ANIMAL JOKES

On what side does a duck have the most feathers?

The outside!

How many skunks does it take to make a stink?

A phew!

What did one pig say to the other?

You take me for grunted!

WHAT DO PIGS PUT ON CUTS?

OINK-MENT!

WHY DID THE EGG HIDE?

IT WAS A LITTLE CHICKEN!

Who tells the funniest egg jokes?
Comedi-hens!

How do chickens leave the building?
They use the eggs-it!

What do you give a poorly kangaroo?
A hop-eration!

ANIMAL JOKES

WHAT DO YOU CALL A DUCK THAT'S ALWAYS TELLING JOKES?

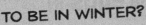 A WISE-**QUACKER**!

WHAT DO YOU GET FROM NERVOUS COWS?

MILKSHAKES!

WHICH ANIMAL DO YOU WANT TO BE IN WINTER?

A LITTLE 'OTTER!

WHAT'S A POLYGON?

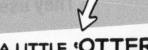 A DEAD PARROT!

HOW DO HORSES SAY HELLO?

HAY!

WHY DID THE ELEPHANTS QUIT THE CIRCUS?

THEY WERE BEING PAID **PEANUTS!**

WHAT'S A BEAR'S FAVOURITE DRINK?

GASSY FIZZ

COCA-**KOALA!**

WHAT ANIMAL DRIVES REALLY BADLY?

A ROAD **HOG!**

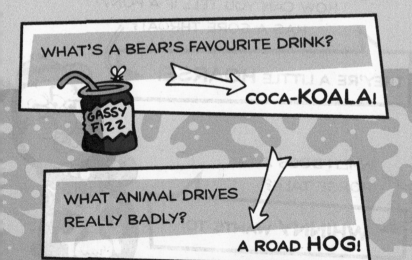

ANIMAL JOKES

WHAT GAME DO HORSES LIKE BEST?

STABLE TENNIS!

WHAT DO YOU ASK A SAD HORSE?

WHY THE **LONG FACE?**

HOW CAN YOU TELL IF A PONY HAS A SORE THROAT?

THEY'RE A LITTLE **HOARSE!**

WHEN DOES A HORSE TALK?

WHINNY WANTS TO!

WHY DID THE HORSE SNEEZE?

THEY HAD **HAY** FEVER!

WHAT'S A HORSE'S FAVOURITE TV SHOW?

NEIGHBOURS!

DID YOU HEAR ABOUT THE SAD HORSE?

THEY TOLD A TALE OF **WHOA**!

WHAT KIND OF HORSE IS GOOD AT SWIMMING?

A **SEA**HORSE!

ANIMAL JOKES

How do rabbits comb their hair?

With a **hare**-brush!

What kind of first aid do mice learn?

Mouse to **mouse** resuscitation!

Why are elephants wrinkled?

Have you tried ironing one?

How do pigs get to hospital?

By **ham**-bulance!

OINK!
HONK!

What did the dog say when it sat on some sandpaper?

Ruff!

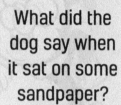

Who stole the soap at bath time?

The **robber** ducky!

What weighs two tons and jumps like a frog?

A **hoppy-potamus**!

Where do kittens go on school trips?

The **mew**-seum!

ANIMAL JOKES

Where do tough chickens come from?

Hard-boiled eggs!

How do rabbits travel?

By **hare**-oplane!

What's a mouse's favourite game?

Hide-and-**squeak!**

What kind of bird sticks to clothes?

A Vel-crow!

What's green and loud?

A froghorn!

How do you stop an
elephant charging?

Take away its credit card!

Why do cows tell jokes?

To a-MOO-se themselves!

What do you call a cow
you can't see?

Ca-MOO-flaged!

ANIMAL JOKES

WHAT DID THE DUCK SAY TO
THE WAITER?

PUT IT ON MY **BILL!**

WHAT WAS THE
PIG DOING IN
THE KITCHEN?

BACON!

WHAT DO YOU
CALL A BEAR
WITH NO EARS?

A B!

WHY DO DOGS RUN
IN CIRCLES?

**IT'S TOO HARD TO
RUN IN SQUARES!**

WHAT'S BLACK, WHITE AND NOISY?

A ZEBRA PLAYING THE DRUMS!

HOW DO PIGS SEND SECRET MESSAGES?

WITH INVISIBLE OINK!

WHY DO BEARS HAVE FUR COATS?

BECAUSE THEY LOOK SILLY WEARING RAINCOATS!

WHEN IS IT BAD LUCK TO SEE A BLACK CAT?

WHEN YOU'RE A MOUSE!

ANIMAL JOKES

Where do you put a criminal sheep?
Behind baas!

Why was the duck arrested?
It was suspected of fowl play!

Why did Smiffy take his dog
to a watchmaker?

It had ticks!

WHY SHOULD YOU BE CAREFUL WHEN IT'S RAINING CATS AND DOGS?

YOU MIGHT STEP IN A **POODLE**!

What's worse than raining cats and dogs?
Hailing taxis!

What do you call a man with a seagull on his head?
Cliff!

How many elephants can you put into an empty stadium?
ONE – after that, it isn't empty!

CREEPY-CRAWLY JOKES

WHAT MAKES SOMEONE
GO HEE HEE HEE...
EEEEEEEEEEEEEK?

THE BEANO'S MINI AND
VERY BEASTLY COLLECTION
OF CREEPY-CRAWLY
JOKES, OF COURSE - AND
IT STARTS RIGHT HERE.

CREEPY-CRAWLY JOKES

WHAT INSECT IS GOOD AT COUNTING?

AN ACCOUNT**ANT**!

WHY DID THE BEE GET MARRIED?

IT FOUND ITS **HONEY**!

WHAT DO BEES CHEW?

BUMBLE-GUM!

WHAT DO YOU CALL A FLY WITH NO WINGS?

A WALK!

WHERE DO WASPS GO ON HOLIDAY?

STING-APORE!

WHAT INSECTS ARE ALWAYS COMPLAINING?

GRUMBLE-BEES!

WHAT HAPPENS IF YOU EAT CATERPILLARS?

YOU GET **BUTTERFLIES** IN YOUR TUMMY!

DID YOU HEAR ABOUT THE DOG WHO WENT TO SEE THE FLEA CIRCUS?

IT STOLE THE SHOW!

CREEPY-CRAWLY JOKES

Why did the spider buy a car?

It wanted to go for a spin!

Why are spiders good swimmers?

They have webbed feet!

What do spiders eat at
fast food restaurants?

French flies!

What has 50 legs but can't walk?

Half a centipede!

How do fireflies say goodbye?
Got to glow!

Why did the ladybird go to the doctor?
It had spots!

How do snails fight?
They slug it out!

CREEPY-CRAWLY JOKES

HOW DO FLEAS GET AROUND?

BY ITCH-HIKING!

WHAT INSECTS ARE THE MOST UNTIDY?

LITTER-BUGS!

WHAT INSECT RUNS AWAY FROM EVERYTHING?

A FLEA!

WHAT CAN FLY UNDERWATER?

A BEE IN A SUBMARINE!

WHAT'S A SNAIL?

A SLUG WITH A CRASH HELMET!

WHERE DO YOU TAKE A POORLY HORNET?

THE **WASP**-ITAL!

WHAT DO BUTTERFLIES SLEEP ON?

CATER-PILLOWS!

ALERT! ALERT! You have reached page 60 and qualified for ONE BONUS JOKE. **Congratulations!**

How do you know the ocean needs a bath?

Because it has a sandy bottom.

Now, grab your rubber ring and dive in to find more under-the-sea jokes!

Why do fish live in salt water?

Pepper makes them sneeze!

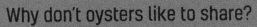

What's the most famous fish?

A starfish!

Why don't oysters like to share?

Because they're shellfish!

UNDER-THE-SEA JOKES

Where do fish sleep?
On the seabed!

What do you call a fish with no eyes?
A fsh!

What's the best way to get in touch with a fish?
Drop it a line!

Why don't fish play tennis?

They're scared of the net!

Why did the octopus cross the road?

To get to the other tide!

What do mussels do on their birthdays?

They SHELL-ebrate!

UNDER-THE-SEA JOKES

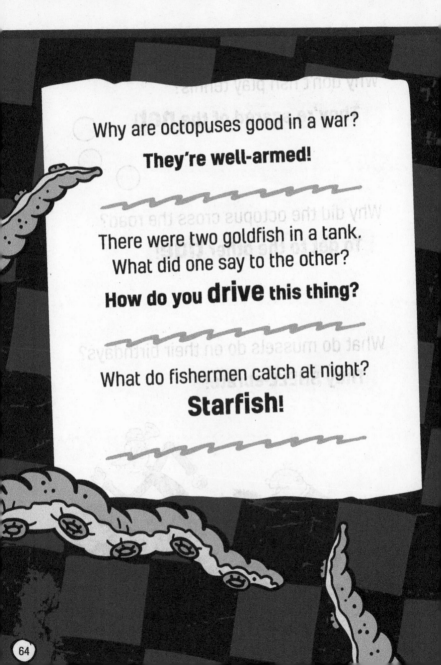

Why are octopuses good in a war?

They're well-armed!

There were two goldfish in a tank.
What did one say to the other?

How do you drive this thing?

What do fishermen catch at night?

Starfish!

WHAT DO FISH USE TO HELP THEM HEAR?

A **HERRING** AID!

What kind of fish performs operations?
A sturgeon!

What's the fastest thing on water?
A motor-pike!

UNDER-THE-SEA JOKES

WHICH PART OF A FISH WEIGHS THE MOST?

THE SCALES!

WHAT DO YOU CALL A SHARK WEARING A TIE?

SO-**FISH**-TICATED!

WHAT SEA CREATURE CAN ADD UP?

AN OCTO-**PLUS!**

WHY WAS THE CRAB ARRESTED?

FOR **PINCHING** STUFF!

WHERE DO WALRUSES GO TO SEE MOVIES?

THE **DIVE-IN!**

HOW DO DOLPHINS MAKE DECISIONS?

THEY **FLIPPER** COIN!

DINOSAUR JOKES

ARE YOU READY FOR JOKES
THAT ARE EVEN OLDER THAN
YOUR GREAT-AUNTIE MYRTLE?
FANTASTIC! BECAUSE WE'VE
TRAVELLED BACK IN TIME TO
DIG UP ENOUGH JURASSIC
JOKES AND CRETACEOUS
CHUCKLES TO MAKE
A T. REX TITTER.
(JUST DON'T LAUGH
AT THEIR TINY
HANDS, OK?)

(THESE JOKES ARE)
BEST BEFORE:
65 MILLION
YEARS BCE.

WHAT DO YOU CALL A SLEEPING T. REX?

A **DINO**-SNORE!

ZZZZZZ
ZZZZZZ

WHAT DO YOU CALL A DINOSAUR WITH NO EYES?

A DOYOUTHINKHESAURUS!

HOW DO YOU KNOW IF THERE'S A DINOSAUR IN YOUR REFRIGERATOR?

THE DOOR WON'T SHUT!

WHAT'S THE BEST WAY TO RAISE A BABY DINOSAUR?

WITH A **CRANE**!

DINOSAUR JOKES

What do cavemen like on their chips?

Dino-sauce!

What does a Triceratops sit on?

Its **TRICERA**-bottom!

What sport is a Brontosaurus good at?

Squash!

What came after the dinosaur?

Its tail!

What's the best thing to do if you see a Tyrannosaurus rex?

Hope they don't see you!

Why did the dinosaur cross the road?

To eat the chicken on the other side!

What do you find on a dinosaur's floor?

Reptiles!

DINOSAUR JOKES

What do you get when a dinosaur sneezes?

Out of the way as quickly as you can!

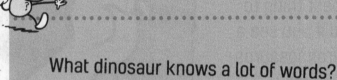

What dinosaur knows a lot of words?

A thesaurus!

Do you know how long dinosaurs lived?

The same as short ones!

What makes more noise than a dinosaur?

Two dinosaurs!

GUZZLE! GORGE! STUFF!

CRAM!

What do you call a Triceratops with carrots in its ears?

Anything you like, it can't hear you!

What do dinosaurs have that no other animals have?

Baby dinosaurs!

Why can't you hear a Pterodactyl using the bathroom?

Because the 'p' is silent!

Why are dinosaurs no longer around?

Because their eggs-stink.

DINOSAUR JOKES

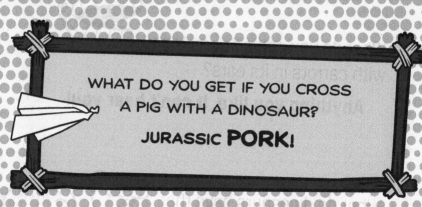

WHAT DO YOU GET IF YOU CROSS
A PIG WITH A DINOSAUR?

JURASSIC **PORK!**

CAN YOU NAME
10 DINOSAURS IN
10 SECONDS?

YES,
8 IGUANODONS
AND
2 STEGOSAURUS!

WHAT DO YOU CALL
A DINOSAUR THAT
NEVER GIVES UP?

TRY-TRY-TRY-
CERATOPS!

DINOSAUR JOKES

WHAT'S AS BIG AS A DINOSAUR BUT WEIGHS NOTHING?

ITS **SHADOW!**

WHY DID THE T. REX EAT RAW MEAT?

BECAUSE ITS **ITTY-BITTY** ARMS COULDN'T WORK THE OVEN.

WHAT SHOULD YOU DO IF YOU FIND A DINOSAUR IN YOUR BED?

FIND SOMEWHERE ELSE TO SLEEP!

DINOSAUR JOKES

What's the difference between a strawberry and a Tyrannosaurus rex?

A strawberry is red!

What weighs 1,600 kilograms and sticks to the roof of your mouth?

A peanut butter and Stegosaurus sandwich!

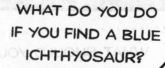

Where do Velociraptors spend their pocket money?

At a dino store!

WHAT DO YOU DO
IF YOU FIND A BLUE
ICHTHYOSAUR?

CHEER THEM UP!

MEGA STINK BOMB

WHEN CAN THREE GIANT DINOSAURS GET UNDER AN UMBRELLA AND NOT GET WET?

WHEN IT'S NOT RAINING!

Who made sure the dinosaurs obeyed the law?

Tricera-cops!

What do you get if you cross a Triceratops with a kangaroo?

A Tricera-hops!

What has a spiked tail, plates on its back and 16 wheels?

A Stegosaurus on roller skates!

DINOSAUR JOKES

WHAT KIND OF DINOSAUR CAN YOU RIDE IN A RODEO?

A **BRONCO**-SAURUS!

WHAT DO YOU CALL A TYRANNOSAURUS REX WHEN IT WEARS A COWBOY HAT AND BOOTS?

TYRANNOSAURUS **TEX**!

WHY DID THE DINOSAUR PAINT ITS TOENAILS RED?

SO THEY COULD HIDE IN THE STRAWBERRY PATCH!

WHAT DO YOU GET WHEN A DINOSAUR WALKS THROUGH A STRAWBERRY PATCH?

STRAWBERRY JAM!

WHAT WAS THE SCARIEST
PREHISTORIC ANIMAL?

THE P-**TERROR**-DACTYL!

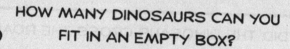

HOW MANY DINOSAURS CAN YOU
FIT IN AN EMPTY BOX?

ONE - AFTER THAT, THE BOX ISN'T EMPTY!

WHY DOES A
BRONTOSAURUS
HAVE A
LONG NECK?

BECAUSE ITS
FEET SMELL.

DINOSAUR JOKES

WHICH DINOSAURS ARE THE WORST DRIVERS?

TYRANNOSAURUS **WRECKS!**

WHY DID THE DINOSAUR CROSS THE ROAD?

BECAUSE CHICKENS HADN'T EVOLVED YET!

WHY DID THE DINOSAUR TAKE A BATH?

TO BE EX-**STINKED!**

WHAT DOES A DINOSAUR CALL A PORCUPINE?

A TOOTHBRUSH!

HOW DOES A T. REX CUT WOOD?

WITH A **DINO**-SAW!

WHAT'S FOUND IN THE MIDDLE OF DINOSAURS?

THE LETTER 'S'!

WHAT DO YOU CALL A DINOSAUR AS TALL AS A HOUSE WITH LONG, SHARP TEETH, AND 12 CLAWS ON EACH FOOT?

SIR.

MENACE SCENE-DO NOT CROSS MENACE SCENE-

CHRISTMAS JOKES

Jingle Bells! It's Christmas!
And if it isn't, don't worry because
it'll be Christmas one day this year.
So put on a party hat, shake your
tinsel and get ready for a selection
of the most fabulously festive
Christmas crackers ever! **YULE***
be laughing before you know it!

*See what we did there?! Oh, never mind.

What do elves learn in school?

The elf-abet!

What do you call someone who's afraid of Santa?

Claus-trophobic!

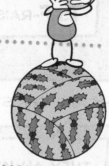

What do frogs love about Christmas?

Mistle-toad!

Who delivers your dog's Christmas presents?

Santa Paws!

CHRISTMAS JOKES

WHAT DOES SANTA USE TO BAKE CAKES?

ELF-RAISING FLOUR!

WHY ARE CHRISTMAS TREES BAD AT SEWING?

THEY ALWAYS DROP THEIR **NEEDLES**!

WHAT'S SANTA'S SISTER CALLED?

MARY CHRISTMAS!

WHAT'S THE WETTEST ANIMAL?

A **RAIN**-DEER!

WHAT HAPPENS TO NAUGHTY ELVES?

THEY GET THE **SACK!**

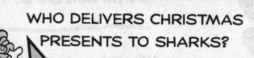

PRESSIEZ FOR MENACEZ

WHAT'S JAMES BOND'S FAVOURITE CHRISTMAS GRUB?

MINCE **SPIES!**

WHO DELIVERS CHRISTMAS PRESENTS TO SHARKS?

SANTA **JAWS!**

WHAT SAYS 'OH OH OH'?

SANTA WALKING BACKWARDS!

CHRISTMAS JOKES

Which reindeer has the worst manners?
Rude-olph!

What do reindeer hang on their Christmas trees?
Horn-aments!

Why does Santa have three gardens?
So he can **hoe, hoe, hoe!**

What do you call Santa when he's on a tea break?
Santa **Pause!**

What's red and white,
red and white, red and white?

Santa rolling down a hill!

How much did Santa pay for his sleigh?

Nothing, it was on the house!

What do you get if Santa forgets
to wear his undercrackers?

Saint Knickerless!

DOCTOR, DOCTOR JOKES

Patient: Doctor, doctor! I've read the *Beano ULTIMATE Joke Book* and learned all of the Doctor, Doctor jokes and now I'm hilarious all of the time.

Doctor: You can't be serious.

(It's true. This book is dangerously funny. Carry on cracking jokes at your own risk.)

Doctor, doctor! I keep thinking
I'm a burglar!

**Have you taken
anything for it?**

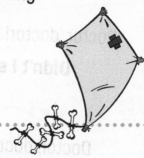

Doctor, doctor! I feel like a pack of cards!

I'll deal with you later!

Doctor, doctor! I think I'm a shepherd!

I wouldn't lose any sheep over it.

Doctor, doctor! What can
you give me for wind?

Nothing, but I can lend you a kite!

DOCTOR, DOCTOR JOKES

Doctor, doctor! I'm suffering from déjà vu!

Didn't I see you yesterday?

Doctor, doctor! I think I'm shrinking!

Calm down and be a little patient!

Doctor, doctor! I keep thinking I'm a dog!

Do take a seat.

I can't – Mum says I'm not allowed on the furniture!

Doctor, doctor! I keep thinking I'm a bell!

Take these and if it's not better soon, give me a ring!

Doctor, doctor! I keep thinking I'm a cat!

How long has this been going on?

Since I was a **kitten**!

Doctor, doctor! Will this cream clear up my spots?

I don't make rash promises!

Doctor, doctor! Everyone thinks I'm a liar!

Oh, I can't believe that!

Doctor, doctor! I keep thinking I'm a bridge!

Goodness, what's come over you?

Ten cars, a tractor and the number 68 bus!

91

DOCTOR, DOCTOR JOKES

Doctor, doctor! I keep seeing spinning insects!

Don't worry, there's a bug going round...

Doctor, doctor! I keep thinking I'm a vampire!

Necks, please!

Doctor, doctor! I think I've lost my memory!

When did this happen?

When did what happen?

Doctor, doctor! I've got a strawberry stuck in my ear!

I've got some cream for that!

Doctor, doctor! I feel like a carrot!

Don't get yourself in a stew!

Doctor, doctor! I've swallowed my pocket money!

Take this and we'll see if there's any change in the morning.

Doctor, doctor! I'm at death's door!

Don't worry, we'll soon pull you through!

Doctor, doctor! I feel so ill, is there no hope?

It depends what you're hoping for!

Doctor, doctor! I feel like a pair of wigwams.

The problem is you're too tents!

Doctor, doctor! I'm addicted to brake fluid.

Nonsense, you can stop anytime.

Doctor, doctor! I couldn't drink my medicine after my bath like you told me.

Why not?

Well after I've drunk my bathwater, I haven't got room for the medicine.

Doctor, doctor! Every time I drink a cup of hot chocolate I get a stabbing pain in the eye.

Try taking the spoon out first.

Doctor, doctor! I feel like a sheep.

Oh that's very baaa-d!

Doctor, doctor! I feel like a pair of curtains.

Pull yourselves together.

Doctor, doctor! I've just swallowed a roll of film!

Come back tomorrow and we'll see what develops!

DOCTOR, DOCTOR JOKES

Doctor, doctor! I think I need glasses.

You certainly do, this is the fish and chip shop!

Doctor, doctor! I'm suffering from insomnia.

Try sleeping at the edge of the mattress, you'll soon drop off.

Doctor, doctor! They've dropped me from the cricket team – they call me butterfingers.

Don't worry, what you have is not catching.

Doctor, doctor! I'm really worried about my breathing.

We'll soon put a stop to that.

Doctor, doctor! People keep ignoring me.

Next, please.

Doctor, doctor, I've got acute appendicitis.

You've got a cute little dimple, too.

Doctor, doctor! What's the quickest way to get to hospital?

Lie in the road outside.

Doctor, doctor! I've only got 59 seconds to live!

Just wait a minute will you...

DOCTOR, DOCTOR JOKES

Doctor, doctor! I've heard that exercise kills germs; is it true?

Probably, but how do you get the germs to exercise?

Doctor, doctor! I've gone all crumbly, like a cheese biscuit.

You're crackers.

Doctor, doctor! You've got to help me – I just can't stop my hands from shaking!

Do you drink lots of fizzy drinks?

Not really – I spill most of it!

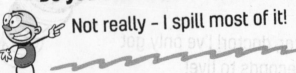

Doctor, doctor! Can I have second opinion?

Of course, come back tomorrow!

Doctor, doctor! I've become invisible.

I'm afraid I can't see you now.

Doctor, doctor! My nose runs and my feet smell.

I fear you might have been built upside down.

Doctor, doctor! I've broken my arm in two places.

Hmm, I'd advise you not to go back to either of those places, then.

Doctor, doctor! I feel like a pony!

Relax, you're just a little hoarse!

DOCTOR, DOCTOR JOKES

Doctor, doctor! You said I'd be dead in ten – ten what? Years? Months?

10, 9, 8, 7, 6...

Doctor, doctor! I've become a kleptomaniac.

Have you taken anything for it?

So far a TV, three sofas and a necklace.

Doctor, doctor! An alternative medicine quack told us to put a LOT of goose fat all over Grandad's back.

If you do that, he'll go downhill fast.

Doctor, doctor! I've swallowed a fish bone.

Are you choking?

No, I really did!

Doctor, doctor! I'm scared of Father Christmas.

You're suffering from Claus-trophobia.

Doctor, doctor! I keep seeing spots before my eyes.

Have you seen a doctor already?

Doctor, doctor! I've a little bit of lettuce sticking out of my bottom.

Oh dear, I'm afraid to say it looks to me like just the tip of the iceberg.

Doctor, doctor! I keep comparing things with something else.

Don't worry, it's only analogy.

DOCTOR, DOCTOR JOKES

Doctor, doctor! I keep thinking
I'm a caterpillar.

Don't worry, you'll soon change...

Doctor, doctor! I can't help thinking I'm a goat.

How long have you felt like this?

Since I was a kid.

Doctor, doctor! Aaa, Eee, I, Ooh! You...

I think you may have irritable vowel syndrome.

Doctor, doctor! I keep singing
'Green, green grass of home' – I think
I have Tom Jones syndrome.

It's not unusual.

Doctor, doctor! I keep thinking I'm a moth.
You need a psychiatrist, not a doctor.

I know, but I was walking past and I saw
your **light was on.**

~~~~~~~~~~

Doctor, doctor! You have to help me out.
Certainly. Which way did you come in?

~~~~~~~~~~

Doctor, doctor! I've got amnesia.
Just go home and try to forget about it.

~~~~~~~~~~

Doctor, doctor! I've got a cricket ball
stuck in my bottom.
How's that?

Oh, don't you start.

FOOD JOKES

YOU'D BUTTER BELIEVE IT...
IT'S THYME FOR FOOD JOKES!
THEY'RE EGG-CELLENT!
THEY'RE SOUP-ERB! THEY'RE
NOT EVEN A TINY BIT CORN-Y.
IN FACT, WE'VE COOKED
UP SO MANY RIB-TICKLING
FOOD JOKES THAT YOU'LL
BE S-PEACH-LESS!

IMPORTANT NOTICE: THE
BEAN-O IS DREADFULLY
SORRY ABOUT THE NUMBER
OF FOOD-RELATED PUNS
ON THIS PAGE.
PLEASE LETTUCE
APOLOGISE.

WHAT KIND OF BAGEL CAN FLY?

A **PLAIN** BAGEL!

WHAT DO YOU GET IF YOU CROSS A CHEETAH WITH A BURGER?

FAST FOOD!

WHAT DO YOU CALL CHEESE THAT DOESN'T BELONG TO YOU?

NACHO CHEESE!

WHY DO BANANAS WEAR SUNSCREEN?

BECAUSE THEY **PEEL**!

FOOD JOKES

WHAT'S ORANGE AND SOUNDS LIKE A PARROT?

A CARROT!

WHAT HAPPENS WHEN AN EGG HEARS A JOKE?

IT **CRACKS** UP!

WHAT DO YOU CALL A FAKE LASAGNE?

AN **IMPASTA!**

WHY DID THE FARMER EAT YEAST AND SHOE POLISH BEFORE THEY WENT TO BED?

SO THEY COULD **RISE** AND **SHINE!**

DID YOU HEAR ABOUT THE SALAD RACE?

THE LETTUCE WAS aHEAD AND THE TOMATO TRIED TO KETCHUP!

WHAT DO YOU EAT WHEN YOU'RE COLD AND ANGRY?

A BRR-GRR!

WHY DID THE BANANA GO TO THE DOCTOR?

HE WASN'T PEELING WELL!

WHAT'S GREEN AND GOES CAMPING?

A BRUSSELS SCOUT!

FOOD JOKES

Dennis: 'This egg is bad!'

Dad: 'Don't blame me, I only laid the table!'

Why did the onion need help?

It was in a pickle!

What's white and giggles?

A tickled onion!

What do you call a fast fungus?

A mush-vroom!

How do you make milkshake?

Give it a good scare!

Why did the orange stop rolling down the hill?

It ran out of juice!

What do you give an injured fruit?

Lemon-aid!

Which cheese is 'made' backwards?

Edam!

FOOD JOKES

WHAT DO YOU CALL A MISCHIEVOUS EGG?

A PRACTICAL **YOLKER!**

WHAT'S THE BEST THING TO PUT IN A PIE?

YOUR **TEETH!**

WHAT FLOWERS MAKE A REALLY BAD GIFT?

CAULIFLOWERS

WHAT'S ANGRY AND GOES WITH CUSTARD?

APPLE **GRUMBLE!**

WHAT DOES A CLOCK DO WHEN IT'S HUNGRY?

IT GOES BACK **FOUR SECONDS**!

WHAT'S THE EASIEST WAY TO MAKE A BANANA SPLIT?

CUT IT IN HALF!

WHAT KIND OF KEY OPENS A BANANA?

A **MON**-KEY!

WHAT DO YOU DO IF YOU SEE A BLUE BANANA?

TRY TO CHEER IT UP!

FOOD JOKES

What did the banana say to the monkey?

Nothing, bananas can't talk!

___

How do you make a sausage roll?

Push it down a hill!

___

What did the egg say to the mixer?

I know when I'm beaten!

___

Why did the tomato blush?

It saw the salad dressing!

How do you start a jelly race?

On your marks, get set!

How do you make the best gold soup?

Use 24-carrots!

EXTRA LARDY CRISPS

Which vegetables go best with jacket potatoes?

Button mushrooms!

Which is the best day to cook bacon?

Fry-day!

FOOD JOKES

When does coffee taste like mud?

When it's ground!

What did the grape do when it was sat on?

Nothing, it just let out a little wine!

Who was the scariest cake?

Attila the Bun!

How do comedians like
their eggs cooked?

Funny side up!

Where do eggs go when they visit the USA?

New Yolk!

What do you call an adventurous egg?

An eggs-plorer!

Why shouldn't you tease egg whites?

They can't take a yolk!

Why are fish and chip shops always full?

Because the fish fillet!

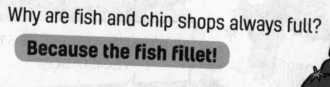

FOOD JOKES

Why did Smiffy eat his homework?

Cuthbert told him it was a piece of cake!

What kind of nut always has a cold?

A cashew!

What vegetables should you never bring on a boat?

Leeks!

FLOUR

WHAT'S THE FASTEST VEGETABLE?

A **RUNNER** BEAN!

WHAT WOBBLES AND FLIES?

A **JELLY**-COPTER!

What's a Canadian's favourite dessert?
Chocolate moose!

What does salad say at church?
Lettuce pray!

What begins with T, ends with T
and has T in it?

A teapot!

FOOD JOKES

WHAT'S A SCARECROW'S FAVOURITE FRUIT?

STRAWBERRIES!

WHAT'S YELLOW AND SNIFFS?

A BANANA WITH A COLD!

WHY ARE BANANAS NEVER LONELY?

THEY HANG AROUND IN BUNCHES!

WHAT'S PURPLE AND HUMS?

A ROTTEN PLUM!

HOW DO YOU KNOW
IF A CAKE IS SAD?

IT'S IN **TIERS**!

WHAT DID ONE SAUSAGE
SAY TO THE OTHER?

YOU'RE THE **WURST**!

WHY DID THE BREAD GO TO THE DOCTOR?

IT WAS FEELING **CRUMMY**!

WHAT'S YELLOW
AND CLICKS?

A BALLPOINT BANANA!

119

Knock,
knock!

Who's there?

Smellmop.

**Smellmop
who?**

Ew!
No thanks!

Knock,
knock!

Who's there?

Spell.

Spell who?

W-H-O!

Knock, knock!
Who's there?
Boo.
Boo who?
No need to cry, it's only a joke!

Knock, knock!
Who's there?
Lettuce.
Lettuce who?
Lettuce in, it's cold out here!

KNOCK, KNOCK JOKES

Knock, knock!
Who's there?
Europe.
Europe who?
No, you're a poo!

Knock, knock!
Who's there?
A broken pencil.
A broken pencil who?
Never mind. It's **pointless**.

Knock, knock!

Who's there?

Al.

Al who?

Al give you a tenner if you open the door!

Knock, knock!

Who's there?

Theodore.

Theodore who?

Theo-dore wasn't open, so I had to knock!

Knock, knock!
Who's there?
Amos.
Amos who?
A mosquito!

Knock, knock!
Who's there?
To.
To who?
Actually,
it's to whom.

KNOCK, KNOCK JOKES

Knock, knock!
Who's there?
The interrupting cow.
The interrupting...
[INTERRUPT THEM]
MOOOO!

Knock, knock!
Who's there?
Little old lady.
Little old lady who?
Wow! I didn't know
you could yodel!

KNOCK, KNOCK JOKES

Knock, knock!

Who's there?

Mikey.

Mikey who?

Mi-key won't open the door!

Knock, knock!

Who's there?

Euripides.

Euripides who?

Eu-ripi-des jeans, you pay for them!

MONSTER JOKES

ARRRRGHHHHHHHHH!

THEY'RE HORRIBLY HILARIOUS AND SCARILY SPOOKY. BUT IF YOU'RE BIG ENOUGH AND BRAVE ENOUGH, READ ON TO DISCOVER SOME OF THE MOST MONSTROUSLY FUNNY JOKES EVER.

WHY DID THE BLOB STAY AT HOME?

HE HAD NO PLACE TO GOO!

WHAT DO YOU USE TO MEND A JACK-O'-LANTERN?

A PUMPKIN **PATCH!**

WHAT'S A BLOB'S FAVOURITE DRINK?

SLIME-ADE!

WHAT DO GHOSTS PUT ON THEIR TURKEY?

GRAVE-Y!

MONSTER JOKES

Why did the witch go to the doctor?

She had a dizzy spell!

How do you make a witch itch?

Take away the 'w'!

Why did the skeleton go to the restaurant?

For spare ribs!

What kind of letters do vampires get?

Fang mail!

What did the daddy ghost say to the baby ghost?

Fasten your sheet belt!

EVIL LEER!

What do you do when 50 ghosts visit your house?

Hope it's Halloween!

Why are ghosts bad at telling lies?

You can see right through them!

What should you say if you meet a ghost?

How do you BOO?

DANGER!

MONSTER JOKES

WHAT DO YOU FIND UP A GHOST'S NOSE?

BOOgers!

HOW DO GHOSTS FLY?

MONSTER SCAREWAYS!

WHAT KIND OF TV DO YOU FIND IN A HAUNTED HOUSE?

WIDE-SCREAM!

WHAT DO SEA MONSTERS EAT?

FISH AND SHIPS!

WHO DID DRACULA GO ON A DATE WITH?

HIS **GHOUL**-FRIEND!

WHAT'S BIG, GREEN AND MOODY?

THE **SULK**!

AFTER IT HAD ITS TEETH TAKEN OUT, WHAT DID THE MONSTER EAT?

THE DENTIST!

WHAT'S THE BEST THING TO GIVE A SEASICK MONSTER?

PLENTY OF ROOM!

MONSTER JOKES

How do monsters like their eggs?

Terri-fried!

Where do you find a monster snail?

At the end of a monster's finger!

What's big, furry and has eight wheels?

A monster on roller skates!

What monster fits on the end of your finger?

The bogeyman!

How can you tell if there's a
monster in your fridge?

You can't shut the door!

Can a monster jump higher than a tree?

Of course – trees can't jump!

What do you do with a green monster?

Wait until it's ripe!

What happens to witches who
break the school rules?

They get ex-spelled!

MONSTER JOKES

On what day do monsters eat people?

Chews-day!

What does a headless horseman ride?

A night-mare!

What do you call witches who lift-share?

Broom-mates!

What tool helps a ghost
to lie perfectly flat?

A spirit level!

How would you describe a monster with amazingly good hearing?

Eerie!

How do monsters count to 13?

On their fingers!

How do vampires get into houses?

Through the bat flap!

How do you get into a locked graveyard?

Use a skeleton key!

MONSTER JOKES

What position does a ghost play in football?

Ghoul-keeper!

Why did the vampire brush its teeth?

It had **bat** breath!

Why do dragons sleep during the day?

So they can fight **knights**!

WHAT DO GHOSTS SAY TO THEIR CHILDREN?

SPOOK WHEN YOU'RE **SPOOKEN** TO!

HOW DO PIXIES EAT?

BY **GOBLIN**!

How does Dracula stay fit?
He plays bat-minton!

Why did the skeleton quit?
Its heart wasn't in it!

MONSTER JOKES

WHY DID THE GHOST GO
TO THE THEATRE?

TO SEE A **PHANTOM**-IME!

WHAT'S DRACULA'S
FAVOURITE DOG?

A BLOODHOUND!

WHAT HAPPENED TO THE
BAD-TEMPERED WITCH?

NEEP-
NEEP

SHE FLEW OFF THE HANDLE!

WHAT GHOSTS HAUNT
HOSPITALS?

SURGICAL **SPIRITS**!

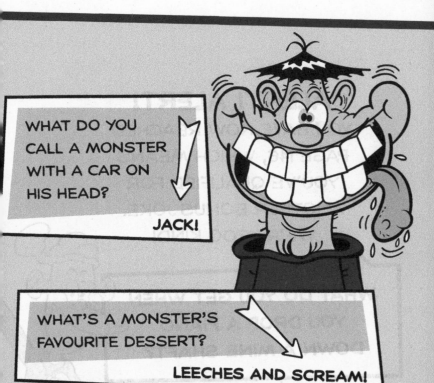

WHAT DO YOU CALL A MONSTER WITH A CAR ON HIS HEAD?

JACK!

WHAT'S A MONSTER'S FAVOURITE DESSERT?

LEECHES AND SCREAM!

WHAT NOISE DID THE WITCH'S CEREAL MAKE?

SNAP, **CACKLE** AND POP!

MUSIC JOKES

ALERT! ALERT!
YOU HAVE NOW REACHED
PAGE 146, WHICH MEANS
YOU'VE QUALIFIED FOR
ANOTHER BONUS JOKE.
WE'RE TOO KIND!

WHAT DO YOU GET WHEN
YOU DROP A PIANO
DOWN A MINE SHAFT?

A FLAT MINER!

NOW GO THIS WAY TO
FIND MORE MUSIC JOKES!

MUSIC JOKES

Which pets make the most noise?

Trum-pets!

What keeps jazz musicians on the floor?

Groov-ity!

Why did Gran put wheels on her rocking chair?

So she could rock 'n' roll!

What has 88 keys but can't open a door?

A piano!

MUSIC JOKES

Which musical instruments can catch fish?

Castanets!

Why did Smiffy keep his trumpet in the fridge?

He liked cool music!

ACE SCENE-DO NOT CROSS   MENACE SCENE-DO NOT C

What do you call a cow who plays guitar?

A moo-sician!

Why are pirates great singers?

They hit the high Cs!

Why did the bee hum?

It didn't know the words!

What makes music on your head?

A hairband!

MUSIC JOKES

WHERE WOULD YOU FIND A RUBBER TRUMPET?

IN AN **ELASTIC** BAND!

WHAT MUSICAL INSTRUMENT IS FOUND IN THE BATHROOM?

A **TUBA** TOOTHPASTE!

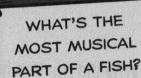

WHAT'S THE MOST MUSICAL PART OF A FISH?

THE **SCALES!**

WHY DON'T COMPOSERS USE EMAIL?

THEY WRITE **NOTES!**

WHY ARE DRUMMERS NEVER LATE?

THEY **BEAT** THE CLOCK!

DID YOU HEAR ABOUT THE MUSIC SHOP ROBBERY?

THIEVES MADE OFF WITH THE **LUTE**!

WHAT'S A SKELETON'S FAVOURITE INSTRUMENT?

A TROM**BONE**!

SCHOOL JOKES

Quiet, please! Pay attention!
Sit up straight and stop picking
your nose. Quit swivelling round in
your chair and don't stare out
of the window because it's time
to go **BACK TO SCHOOL**.
We're not even joking!*

* Well, we are. Obviously.
It's a joke book.

WHY WAS THE MATHS BOOK SAD?
IT HAD TOO MANY **PROBLEMS!**

Where do library books like to sleep?

Under their covers!

What happened to the maths teacher's garden?

The plants all grew square roots!

Why should you never do maths in the jungle?

Because if you add four and four, you might get 'ate'!

SCHOOL JOKES

WHY WAS THE MUSIC TEACHER SAD?

HE HAD LOTS OF **TREBLES!**

WHAT'S A SNAKE'S FAVOURITE SUBJECT?

HISSTORY!

WHY DID THE MUSIC TEACHER NEED A LADDER?

TO REACH THE **HIGH NOTES!**

WHY IS AN ENGLISH
TEACHER LIKE
A JUDGE?

THEY BOTH HAND
OUT **LONG
SENTENCES!**

...

WHY WAS THE
TEACHER
CROSS-EYED?

THEY COULDN'T
CONTROL THEIR
PUPILS!

HOW DO YOU GET
STRAIGHT 'A'S
AT SCHOOL?

USE A
RULER!

...

SCHOOL JOKES

SCRAWNY SQUELCH!

WHY DID THE TEACHER GO TO THE BEACH?

THEY WANTED TO TEST THE WATER!

WHAT DO BUTTERFLIES STUDY AT SCHOOL?

MOTH-ematics!

MEGA STINK BOMB

WHY DID THE TEACHER WRITE ON THE WINDOW?

SO THEIR LESSON WAS CLEAR!

WHY DID THE ECHO GET DETENTION?

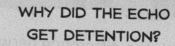

FOR ANSWERING BACK!

SLURP! BURP!

TYPE "O"

WHAT DO YOU GET IF YOU CROSS A TEACHER WITH A VAMPIRE?

A **BLOOD** TEST!

WHAT'S BLACK, WHITE AND HORRIBLE?

A **MATHS** TEST!

SCHOOL JOKES

What's the difference between teachers and sweets?

Kids like sweets!

Who's in charge of the pencil case?
The ruler!

What did one pencil say to the other pencil?
You're looking sharp!

Why shouldn't you write with a broken pencil?

It's **pointless**!

How do bees get to school?

On the **school buzz**!

What's the worst thing you can find in a school canteen?

The food!

SILLY JOKES

DEAR TRAINEE COMEDIAN,

ARE YOU:
A) AS DOTTY AS A DOMINO?
B) AS DAFT AS A BRUSH?
C) RIDICULOUS WITH A CAPITAL R?

YOU ARE? ALL THREE?!
THEN... CONGRATULATIONS!
THESE SUPREMELY SILLY JOKES
HAVE BEEN WRITTEN JUST FOR YOU.

YOURS FOOLISHLY,
BEANO

DID YOU HEAR ABOUT THE WOMAN WHO WORE SUNGLASSES?

SHE TOOK A VERY **DIM VIEW** ON THINGS!

WHAT DID ONE BOGEY SAY TO THE OTHER?

YOU THINK YOU'RE FUNNY, BUT YOU'RE **SNOT!**

BELCH! BAARP!

HOW DO YOU MAKE A TISSUE DANCE?

PUT A LITTLE **BOOGIE** IN IT!

WHAT DID ONE TOILET SAY TO THE OTHER?

YOU LOOK A LITTLE **FLUSHED!**

SILLY JOKES

Why don't farts do well at school?
They get expelled!

What's the smelliest city in America?
Phew York!

Why did the cup go to the police?
It was mugged!

Did you hear about the thief who
stole a surfboard?

**He escaped on a
crime wave!**

Did you hear about the man who was arrested for being an art thief?

He was framed!

What did the police officer say to their tummy?

You're under a-vest!

Why was the belt arrested?

It held up some trousers!

What three letters frighten burglars?

I-C-U!

SILLY JOKES

What nails do carpenters hate to hit?

Finger nails!

What do lawyers wear to court?

Law suits!

What month do soldiers hate the most?

March!

Why did the computer break up
with the Internet?

There was no connection!

Why did Smiffy throw the clock out of the window?

He wanted to see time fly!

How do farmers mend their trousers?

With cabbage patches!

What kind of shoes do spies wear?

Sneakers!

Why did Smiffy run around his bed?

He wanted to catch up on his sleep!

SILLY JOKES

How does a train eat?

Chew-chew!

Why is six afraid of seven?

Because seven 'eight' nine!

What's a trampoline's favourite season?

Spring!

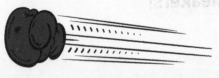

WHERE DID THE KING KEEP HIS ARMIES?

UP HIS **SLEEVIES!**

WHAT'S A PIRATE'S FAVOURITE LETTER?

ARRR!

Why did the burglar take a bath?

He wanted to make a clean getaway!

How do you cut a wave in half?

Use a sea-saw!

What did the pirate say on his 80th birthday?

Aye-matey!

SILLY JOKES

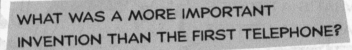

WHAT WAS A MORE IMPORTANT INVENTION THAN THE FIRST TELEPHONE?

THE SECOND TELEPHONE!

WHY DID THE PICTURE GO TO JAIL?

BECAUSE IT WAS FRAMED!

WHY DID THE COMPUTER GO TO THE DOCTOR?

IT HAD A VIRUS!

WHAT DO YOU CALL A FUNNY MOUNTAIN?

HILL-ARIOUS!

WHAT WAS WRONG WITH THE WOODEN CAR?

IT **WOODEN** GO!

WHAT DID ONE OCEAN SAY TO THE OTHER OCEAN?

NOTHING, IT JUST **WAVED!**

WHAT TREMBLES AT THE BOTTOM OF THE OCEAN?

A NERVOUS **WRECK!**

WHY WAS THE SAND WET?

BECAUSE THE SEA**WEED!**

SILLY JOKES

WHAT SECRET AGENT LIVES IN A
BOTTLE OF WASHING-UP LIQUID?

BUBBLE-07!

WHAT MONTH DO TREES HATE MOST?

SEP-TIMBERRR!

WHAT'S THE CUTEST SEASON?

AWWWW-TUMN!

WHAT DID ONE LEAF SAY
TO ANOTHER?

I'M FALLING FOR YOU!

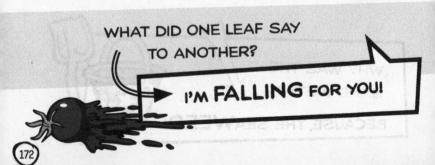

WHY DID THE TREE GET IN TROUBLE?

IT WAS **KNOTTY!**

WHAT DID THE LITTLE TREE SAY TO THE BIG TREE?

LEAF ME ALONE!

WHY DO TREES HATE TESTS?

THEY HATE BEING **STUMPED!**

WHAT DO TREES SAY WHEN WINTER IS OVER?

THAT'S A RE-**LEAF!**

SILLY JOKES

Which painting complains a lot?

The Moaner Lisa!

What's the tallest building in the world?

The library. It has the most stories!

Why did the driver check their tyres for punctures?

Because there was a fork in the road!

What do you call a belt with a watch on?

A waist of time!

Why is it fun to play jokes on Humpty Dumpty?

He always **falls** for it!

Why did the man put lipstick on his forehead?

He wanted to **make-up** his mind!

What washes up on very small beaches?

Micro**waves**!

Why are pirates called pirates?

Just because they **arrr**!

SILLY JOKES

Why are perfume sellers really smart?

They have lots of common scents!

Why couldn't the bike stand up?

It was two tyred.

What's the best time to go the dentist?

Two thirty!

What did the hat say to the scarf?

You hang around, I'll go on ahead!

Why don't people get married in igloos?

In case they get cold feet!

How do you know if a snowman
has been in your bed?

You wake up wet.

How do you sink Smiffy's submarine?

Knock on the door!

What do farmers do when they're tired?

They hit the hay!

SILLY JOKES

HOW DO YOU START A CUDDLY TOY RACE?

READY, **TEDDY**, GO!

WHY ARE MEDIEVAL TIMES CALLED THE DARK AGES?

BECAUSE THERE WERE A LOT OF **KNIGHTS!**

WHAT TOY HATES TO BE PICKED UP?

LEGGO!

WHY DID THE TRAFFIC LIGHT TURN RED?

PEOPLE SAW IT **CHANGING!**

WHAT FLOWER GROWS ON YOUR FACE?

TULIPS!

WHAT DID THE BLANKET SAY TO THE BED?

I'VE GOT YOU COVERED!

WHAT HAPPENED WHEN THE TV AERIALS GOT MARRIED?

THEY HAD A GREAT **RECEPTION!**

WHY WAS THE ARCHAEOLOGIST SAD?

THEIR CAREER WAS IN **RUINS!**

SILLY JOKES

What's the hardest thing about
learning to ride a bike?

The ground!

How do robots drive?

They put their metal to the pedal!

Why did the axe go to the doctor?

It had a splitting head!

WHY DID THE TAILOR
GO TO THE DOCTOR?

HE HAD
PINS AND
NEEDLES!

WHAT DID THE ZERO
SAY TO THE EIGHT?
NICE BELT!

WORM
YOGHURT

Why did the weightlifter eat bricks?
To build herself up!

Who invented fire?
Some bright spark!

Why did Smiffy eat coins?
It was his lunch money!

SILLY JOKES

WHICH ROMAN
EMPEROR HAD
HAY FEVER?

WHY DID THE MAGNET
GO ON LOTS OF DATES?

JULIUS
SNEEZER!

HE WAS VERY
ATTRACTIVE!

WHY DO BOATS
GO ON DATES?

HOW DO CAVEMEN
SAY I LOVE YOU?

THEY'RE LOOKING
FOR **ROW**-MANCE!

WITH UGS
AND KISSES!

WHERE DOES TARZAN BUY HIS CLOTHES?

—

JUNGLE SALES!

WHY SHOULDN'T YOU USE PAPER PLATES?

—

THEY'RE **TEARABLE!**

WHAT'S A SUPERHERO'S FAVOURITE PART OF A JOKE?

—

THE **PUNCHLINE!**

WHAT DO HEROES PUT IN THEIR DRINKS?

—

JUST ICE!

SILLY JOKES

WHO WAS THE FIRST UNDERWATER SPY?

JAMES **POND!**

WHAT DID THE TORNADO SAY TO THE CAR?

FANCY GOING FOR A **SPIN?**

WHAT HAS TWO WHEELS AND FLIES?

A **WHEELIE** BIN!

WHAT'S THE BIGGEST CAUSE OF
ROAD RAGE?

CROSS-ROADS!

WHY WAS SMIFFY BAD AT HITCH-HIKING?

HE WENT EARLY TO AVOID THE TRAFFIC!

WHAT DANCE DO TIN OPENERS DO?

THE **CAN-CAN!**

WHAT GOES 'HICK-HOCK'?

A CLOCK WITH HICCUPS!

WHY DID THE TAP DANCER GIVE UP?

THEY KEPT FALLING IN THE **SINK!**

SILLY JOKES

Why do hairdressers make good taxi drivers?

They know all the shortcuts!

Why did the lightning get in trouble?

It didn't know how to conduct itself!

Which country is the slipperiest?

Greece!

Why was the nose tired?

It never stopped running!

What do you get when you cross a river and a stream?

Wet!

Did you hear the joke about the dustbin?
It's a load of rubbish!

How did the Vikings send secret messages?

Norse code!

SILLY JOKES

WHAT DO YOU CALL A BOY WITH
A SPADE ON HIS HEAD?

DOUG!

WHEN IS A GREEN BOOK NOT GREEN?

WHEN IT'S READ!

DID YOU HEAR THE JOKE
ABOUT THE BED?

I HAVEN'T MADE IT YET!

WHAT'S ROUND AND DANGEROUS?

A **VICIOUS** CIRCLE!

WHEN IS A DOOR NOT A DOOR?

WHEN IT'S **AJAR**!

WHAT DID THE SHY PEBBLE SAY?

I WISH I WAS A LITTLE **BOULDER**!

WHAT'S THE FASTEST COUNTRY
IN THE WORLD?

RUSH-A!

SILLY JOKES

Why did Pie Face sprinkle sugar on his pillows?

He wanted to have sweet dreams

What type of button can't you buy in shops?

Belly buttons!

Who gets the sack every time he goes to work?

The postman!

Which trees are the handiest?
Palm trees!

When is a sailor not a sailor?
When he's a board!

What's brown and sticky?
A stick!

Why did the taxi driver lose their job?
They kept driving their customers away!

SILLY JOKES

How do mountains hear things?

With mountain-ears!

What house weighs the least?

A lighthouse!

What has fifty legs but can't walk?

25 pairs of trousers!

Why did the human cannonball leave the circus?

He got fired!

FROM A FRIEND

What do you call a really good plumber?

A drain surgeon!

What happened when nineteen and twenty played a game?

Twenty won!

SILLY JOKES

What happens if you spit
out a light bulb?

You're delighted!

What do you call a French person
wearing sandals?

Philippe-Philoppe

What's the coldest country?
Chile!

WHAT CLOTHES DO HOUSES WEAR?

ad**DRESSES!**

What did one wall say to the other wall?
I'll meet you at the corner!

What's soft and slippery?
A slipper!

What flies around waving the
Stars and Stripes?
A USA!

195

SILLY JOKES

WHY IS TUTANKHAMUN ALWAYS BOASTING?

HE **SPHINX** HE'S THE BEST!

HOW DO PIRATES GET TO THE AIRPORT?

THEY RENT A C-**ARRR**!

WHAT DOES THE QUEEN DO WHEN SHE BURPS?

SHE ISSUES A ROYAL PARDON!

WHAT'S KING ARTHUR'S FAVOURITE GAME?

KNIGHTS AND CROSSES!

WHAT'S AN INKLING?

A BABY PEN!

WHY WAS THE BOY SCOUT DIZZY?

HE SPENT THE WHOLE DAY DOING **GOOD TURNS**!

WHAT DO YOU CALL A MAN WITH GRAVY AND POTATOES ON HIS HEAD?

STEW!

HOW DO SNOWMEN GET TO WORK?

BY **ICICLE**!

SILLY JOKES

WHAT HAS A BOTTOM AT THE TOP?

YOUR LEGS!

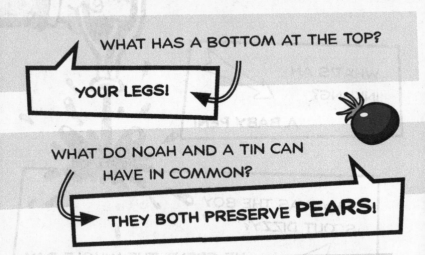

WHAT DO NOAH AND A TIN CAN
HAVE IN COMMON?

THEY BOTH PRESERVE **PEARS!**

WHAT DO PEOPLE MOST OFTEN OVERLOOK?

THEIR NOSES!

MENACE SCENE - DO NOT CR

WHAT GOES BLACK, WHITE, BLACK, WHITE, BLACK, WHITE?

A NUN ROLLING DOWN A HILL!

HOW DO YOU MAKE VARNISH DISAPPEAR?

TAKE AWAY THE 'R'!

WHY IS YOUR MUM'S SISTER GOOD FOR CUTS?

SHE'S **AUNTIE**-SEPTIC!

MENACE SCENE - DO NOT CROS

SILLY JOKES

What's the best day to go to the beach?

Sunday, of course!

What bow can't be tied?

A **rain**bow!

Where do snowmen keep their money?

In snow **banks**!

What do snowmen do in summer?

Chill out!

What gets wetter the more it dries?

A towel!

What's the longest word?

Smiles – there's a mile between the first and last letters!

What do clouds wear beneath their trousers?

Thunder-wear!

What did the icy road say to the truck?

Want to go for a **spin?**

SILLY JOKES

What is the shortest month?

May – it only has three letters!

Why are shoemakers kind?

They have good soles!

What goes up and down
but doesn't move?

A flight of stairs!

What's always on the ground
but doesn't get dirty?

Your shadow!

What has four eyes and a mouth?

The Mississippi!

What can you make that can't be seen?

A noise!

SILLY JOKES

WHY IS GREAT BRITAIN SO WET?

BECAUSE THE QUEEN HAS **REIGNED** FOR DECADES!

CAN FEBRUARY MARCH?

NO, BUT **APRIL MAY!**

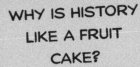

WHY IS HISTORY LIKE A FRUIT CAKE?

IT'S FULL OF **DATES!**

WHY DO SHOES ALWAYS COME IN PAIRS?

THEY'RE **SOLE**-MATES!

HOW ARE FEET
LIKE ANCIENT
STORIES?

THEY'RE
LEGENDS!

WHAT DID THE WALLPAPER SAY
TO THE WALL?

I'VE GOT YOU **COVERED**!

HOW DO TREES GET ON THE INTERNET?

BY **LOGGING** IN!

SPACE JOKES

In space, no one can hear you laugh...

Which is why Earth is the perfect place to blast your friends with the best jokes in the galaxy! And here they all are, clustered in one cosmic chapter.

(Thankfully, we didn't run OUTER SPACE. Ha ha haaaa.)

WHAT KIND
OF MUSIC DO
PLANETS LIKE?

NEP-TUNES!

What did the alien say to the flower bed?

Take me to your weeder!

What's the best way to organise
a space party?

Planet early!

SPACE JOKES

WHAT HAPPENS TO NAUGHTY ASTRONAUTS?

THEY GET **GROUNDED!**

WHAT COMES FROM ANOTHER WORLD AND IS REALLY, REALLY SLOW?

SN-ALIENS!

WHERE DO ASTRONAUTS LEAVE THEIR SPACESHIPS?

AT PARKING **METEORS!**

WHAT CAME FROM
OUTER SPACE TO DO
MAGIC TRICKS?

A FLYING
SORCEROR!

HOW DOES
THE MAN IN THE
MOON CUT
HIS HAIR?

ECLIPSE IT!

WHY WASN'T
THE ASTRONAUT
HUNGRY?

THEY'D HAD A
BIG **LAUNCH!**

SPACE JOKES

WHAT DO YOU CALL A PISTACHIO ON A SPACESHIP?

AN ASTRO-**NUT**!

WHAT DO YOU CALL ALIEN EGGS?

EGGSTRA-TERRESTRIALS!

WHAT DO YOU CALL AN ALIEN WITH THREE EYES?

AN **ALIIIEN**!

WHEN DO ASTRONAUTS EAT?

LAUNCH TIME!

WHAT DO YOU CALL A SPACESHIP THAT DRIPS WATER?

A **CRYING SAUCER!**

WHY DID THE MOON BURP?

BECAUSE IT WAS **FULL!**

SPORTS JOKES

We're **RUNNING** out of pages in this joke book! It's a **SPRINT** to the finish line! RACE to the next page to find the best SPORTS JOKES ever.

Peowwwwwwwww!

Why can't Cinderella play football?

Her coach is a pumpkin!

Why should you never tell a joke when ice skating?

In case the ice cracks up!

Why is tennis such a loud game?

Because every player raises a racket!

Why do golfers wear two pairs of shorts?

In case they get a hole in one!

SPORTS JOKES

WHICH FOOTBALL TEAM LOVES ICE CREAM?

ASTON **VANILLA**!

ARE LIGHTNING BOLTS GOOD AT FOOTBALL?

NO, THEY'RE **SHOCKING**!

WHY COULDN'T CINDERELLA PLAY CRICKET?

SHE ALWAYS RAN AWAY FROM THE **BALL**!

WHAT'S THE CHILLIEST FOOTBALL GROUND?

COLD TRAFFORD!

WHAT KIND OF RACE IS NEVER RUN?

A **SWIMMING** RACE!

WHY COULDN'T THE CAR PLAY FOOTBALL?

IT ONLY HAD ONE **BOOT!**

WHY ARE BASKETBALL PLAYERS MESSY EATERS?

THEY'RE ALWAYS **DRIBBLING!**

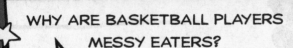

HOW DO FOOTBALLERS STAY COOL?

THEY SIT NEXT TO THEIR **FANS!**

MY OWN JOKES

So that's it! You've memorised over 600 jokes and now you're ready to start being a comedy genius. You're also qualified to start writing your own brilliant jokes on the following pages, which we have helpfully left blank. And, because we're so thoughtful here's one to get you started. You can swap the underlined words for almost anything you like and it'll still be funny. Genius, eh?!

What do you call a <u>Bash Street Kid</u> with <u>Brussels sprouts</u> in their ears?

Anything you like.
They can't hear you!

MY OWN JOKES